MW00953841

2707

DATE DUE

DEMCO, INC. 38-2971

Discovering Science

ROCKS, MINERALS, AND FOSSILS

Rebecca Hunter

**RAINTREE
STECK-VAUGHN
PUBLISHERS**

A Harcourt Company

Austin   New York
www.steck-vaughn.com

Published by Raintree Steck-Vaughn Publishers, an imprint of Steck-Vaughn Company

Acknowledgments
Project Editors: Rebecca Hunter, Pam Wells
Art Director: Max Brinkmann
Illustrated by Pamela Goodchild, Stefan Chabluk, and Keith Williams
Designed by Ian Winton

Planned and produced by Discovery Books

Library of Congress Cataloging-in-Publication Data

Hunter, Rebecca (Rebecca K. de C.)
Rocks, minerals, and fossils / Rebecca Hunter.
p. cm. — (Discovering science)
Includes bibliographical references and index.
ISBN 0-7398-3250-6
1. Rocks—Juvenile literature. 2. Minerals—Juvenile literature.
3. Fossils—Juvenile literature. [Rocks. 2. Minerals. 3. Fossils.] I. Title.

QE432.2 H76 2001
552—dc21
00-042457

CIP AC

2 3 4 5 6 7 8 9 0 BNG 05 04 03 02
Printed and bound in the United States of America.

Note to the reader: You will find difficult words in the glossary on page 30.

CONTENTS

A ROCKY WORLD

We live in a rocky world. We are surrounded by rocks. Rocks cover the whole Earth. They are even under the oceans. No matter where you live, you live on rock. Much of the time we cannot see the rock. It is covered with soil and plants, towns, and cities.

Where rocks are exposed on Earth's surface, we can see them. At the coast you see rocks where they meet the ocean as cliffs or beaches. On mountainsides where the soil is very thin, you can see the rock poking through.

USING ROCK

Rock has many uses. We build walls with it, make roads with it, and construct all sorts of buildings with it. Most of our chemicals and metals also come from rocks.

The Great Pyramid at Giza, Egypt was built about 4,500 years ago. It took over 20 years to build and contains over 6 million tons of rock.

DESCRIBING ROCK

There are many different types of rock. For example, rocks come in many colors. There are gray rocks, black rocks, and pure white ones. There are yellow rocks, red rocks, and pink rocks.

Some rocks are soft and crumbly. Some are hard and strong. Chalk is a very soft rock. This makes it useful for writing on chalkboards. It can easily be rubbed off afterwards.

FOSSILS

Some rocks contain the remains of animals and plants that lived millions of years ago. These rocks are called fossils. Studying fossils can tell us a lot about the history of life on Earth.

ROCKS FROM OUTER SPACE

A small number of the rocks on Earth were not formed here at all. Meteorites are pieces of rock or metal materials from outer space that fall to Earth.

INSIDE THE EARTH

Nobody is certain what the inside of Earth is like below the surface. Scientists believe that it is made up of three main layers, something like a round egg.

At the very center of Earth is the core. The core has an inner solid layer and an outer liquid layer. The inner core is made of the metals iron and nickel and is very, very hot. Together, the inner and outer core are about 2,800 miles (4,480 kilometers) thick.

Lava shoots into the air from Kilauea, a volcano in Hawaii. Lava is molten rock from within Earth.

Surrounding the core is the mantle, which makes up most of the planet. It is about 1,800 miles (2,900 kilometers) thick and is made from hot rocky material. Some of this rock is solid and some is liquid.

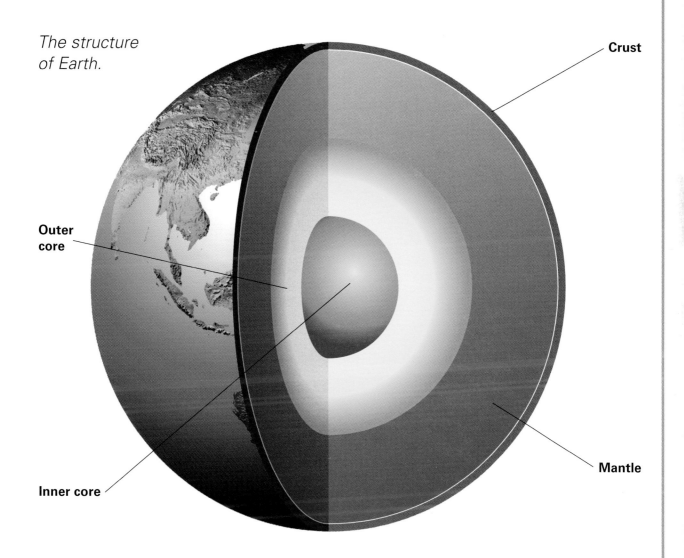

The structure of Earth.

Crust

Outer core

Inner core

Mantle

Covering the mantle is Earth's crust. This is very thin, like the shell on an egg. The crust is much cooler than the mantle. The crust is between 3 and 43 miles (5 and 70 kilometers) thick.

MINERALS

All the rocks in the world are made up of minerals. There are about 3,000 kinds of minerals in Earth's crust. Quartz is one of the most common minerals. It is found in several forms: as sand on the beach, as hard rocks called flints, and as crystals in rocks.

Some rocks contain only one mineral. For example, chalk contains only calcium carbonate.

The famous white cliffs of Dover in England are made of soft chalk.

Other rocks are made up of several minerals. The rock granite, for example, always contains two minerals, quartz and feldspar.

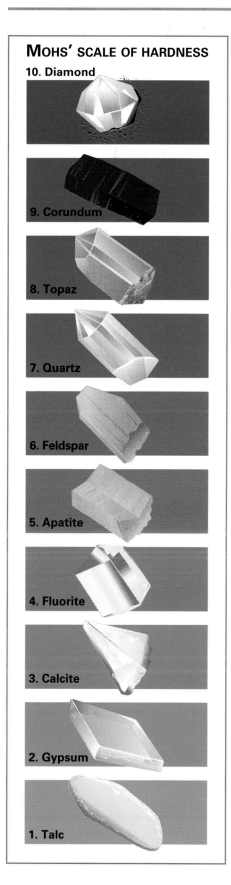

MOHS' SCALE OF HARDNESS

10. Diamond

9. Corundum

8. Topaz

7. Quartz

6. Feldspar

5. Apatite

4. Fluorite

3. Calcite

2. Gypsum

1. Talc

HARDNESS OF MINERALS

Minerals can be identified by their hardness. A German scientist called Friedrich Mohs invented a scale of hardness. He listed ten minerals from the softest (talc) to the hardest (diamond). Each mineral on Mohs' scale can scratch a mineral with a lower number, or be scratched by a mineral with a higher number.

DIAMONDS

The hardest natural mineral is diamond. Diamonds have always been in great demand as jewelry, but far more diamonds are used in industry. Since they are so hard, diamonds are used for cutting in drills and for polishing other hard minerals.

The largest diamond ever found was the Cullinan stone from South Africa. It weighed about 22 ounces (625 grams) and was presented to King Edward VII of Britain in 1907.

CRYSTALS

Most solids, including metals, are made up of crystals. Usually these are too small to be seen, but you can often see them in rocks. Crystals in rocks often have no definite shape because they are packed together. But sometimes they form in rock cavities and make strange and beautiful shapes.

PRECIOUS STONES

Gemstones such as rubies, emeralds, and sapphires are also crystals. They make beautiful jewelry, and they are often very expensive because they are so rare.

Crystals grow in many shapes. You can see how they form by growing some yourself at home.

PROJECT

Grow your own crystals

You will need
Powdered alum (See page 31.)
Food coloring
Hot water
A saucer
A glass jar
A teaspoon
Some thread
A pencil or small stick

1. Put one heaping teaspoon of alum in a jar. Add 2-3 tablespoons of hot water and stir until the powder has dissolved. Leave the solution for at least three hours or overnight to completely cool.

2. Pour the solution into the saucer and leave it uncovered for about 12 hours.

3. When most of the water has evaporated, you will see some crystals of alum left behind on the saucer. Pick the biggest of these, and tie the thread around it. Tie the other end of the thread to the pencil.

4. Make up some more alum solution in the jar, using about 4 heaping teaspoons of alum and filling the jar about two-thirds full of hot water. Keep adding the alum until no more will dissolve. Add a few drops of food coloring. Leave the jar in a cool place for a few hours.

5. Hang the crystal inside the jar. Rest the pencil across the top of the jar to keep the crystal covered with the solution.

6. Leave the jar for a few days in a place where the temperature does not vary much. Then watch your crystal grow!

METALS IN ROCKS

Metals are another type of mineral found in rocks. Rocks containing useful metals are called ores. For the metal to be used, it has to be separated, or extracted, from the ore. Early peoples learned how to extract metals, such as copper and tin, from their ores using heat. This process of taking metal out of ore is called smelting.

These early peoples discovered that they could smelt a mixture of copper and tin ores. This way they could make a stronger metal called bronze.

The ancient Celts made this shield and helmet from bronze.

IRON

Iron is one of the most important metals to humans. It is found in many rocks. It is the second most common element and also the most used and cheapest.

Iron is extracted from iron ore. Most iron is then made into steel. Mining iron ore is an important industry. Most iron is mined through what is called surface mining, which is also sometimes called strip mining or open pit mining. Huge machines and even explosives are used to strip away surface soil and rocks to get at the iron ore below. This process can be very harmful to the environment.

This gold-mining operation in Montana shows what surface mining can do to the land.

PRECIOUS METALS

Like gemstones, some metals are rare and expensive. Gold, silver, and platinum are such precious metals. They are used to make many products. Because of their value and beauty, they are also used to make jewelry.

Gold nuggets are sometimes found in gravel or sand.

TYPES OF ROCKS

Rocks form in different ways. There are three main types of rock—igneous, metamorphic, and sedimentary.

IGNEOUS ROCKS

Most of Earth's crust is made of igneous rock. Igneous means "made by fire." Igneous rocks are formed deep within Earth's crust or mantle, where temperatures are extremely hot. They are formed from molten material called magma.

Granite is an igneous rock. Its crystals are so large they can be seen easily.

VOLCANOES

One way that igneous rock is formed is when molten rock escapes from the crust to the surface and cools down quickly. The molten rock escapes through a vent or opening in the the crust called a volcano.

The molten rock that flows out of a volcano is called lava. As the lava cools it becomes solid. Obsidian, perlite, and basalt are three kinds of rocks formed in this way.

IGNEOUS LANDSCAPES

As igneous rocks form, they take some interesting shapes. We can only see them when the surrounding rocks have been worn away.

The Giant's Causeway in Northern Ireland is made of basalt, a type of rock formed from quick-cooling lava.

Most igneous rocks are very hard and are therefore very useful for building. They are also used to make road surfaces, as when granite or basalt chippings are added to asphalt.

FLOATING ROCK?

A rock that floats? Pumice is a type of igneous rock. It forms from the frothy scum on a lava flow that has gas bubbles trapped in it. It is therefore a very light rock and sometimes will even float on water. People use it to clean things.

SEDIMENTARY ROCKS

Over many years, rocks are broken up into tiny particles. These particles are carried away by wind and water. Finally, they reach a lake or the ocean, where they settle as sediment. Over many years, layer upon layer of sediments are laid down. The weight of the top layers presses down on the lower layers. Slowly, over millions of years, the soft sands or mud are pressed into hard rock.

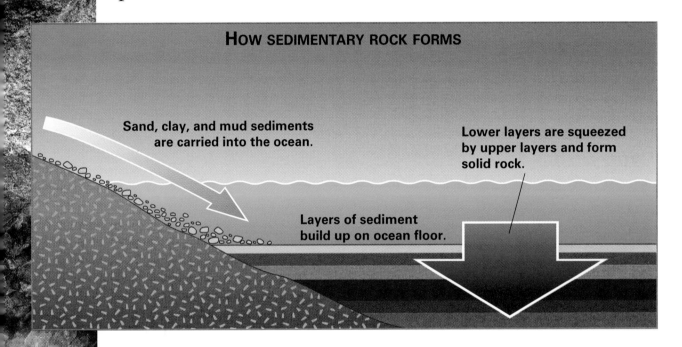

HOW SEDIMENTARY ROCK FORMS

Sand, clay, and mud sediments are carried into the ocean.

Lower layers are squeezed by upper layers and form solid rock.

Layers of sediment build up on ocean floor.

LIMESTONE

Some sedimentary rocks are formed from the remains of living creatures. When corals and shellfish die, they sink to the bottom of the sea. Layers of their skeletons and shells pile up on top of each other. Over millions of years the pressure squeezes the sediments and forms a white or gray rock called limestone. Chalk is a very pure form of limestone.

The layers of sedimentary rocks can still be seen. Look for them at the coast or where roads cut through hills. These layers of rock are called strata. Most rock strata are horizontal when they are formed. Over time they can be folded into wavy patterns.

Layers of sedimentary rock can be seen in this formation in Utah.

PROJECT

Make a rock strata section

You will need
Modeling clay in 4 or 5 different colors
A knife

1. Flatten each ball of clay into a flat disk.

2. Pile the disks up in layers.

3. Each layer represents a different sediment being laid down.

4. Gently push or fold the slab of clay into a different shape.

5. Ask an adult to cut through the clay.

6. The patterns in the layers that you see are similar to those that can be found naturally in rock strata.

METAMORPHIC ROCKS

The third kind of rock in the Earth's crust is called metamorphic rock. Metamorphic means "changed in form." Metamorphic rocks are rocks that have been changed by strong forces underground. There are two forces at work: extreme heat and extreme pressure.

SLATE FROM SHALE

Slate is a metamorphic rock. It was once a sedimentary rock called shale. Over millions of years, tons and tons of rock pressed down on it. This pressure made the shale very hot, and the heat and pressure changed it to slate. Slate is usually black or dark gray. It is shiny and splits easily into thin slices. Because of this people have found it useful for making shingles to cover the roofs of buildings.

Marble

The best-known metamorphic rock is marble. Marble is formed when the sedimentary rock limestone is heated. This often happens in areas around volcanoes.

▶ *Heavy equipment moves stone at a marble quarry in Italy.*

▼ *The famous statue of Abraham Lincoln at the Lincoln Memorial was carved from marble.*

Marble is very hard and often has beautiful colors and markings within it. This makes it a good building material. It can be carved and polished into sculptures or made into tiles to decorate buildings.

FOSSILS

Fossils are the remains or traces of living things in rocks. Fossils form over millions of years. A fossil may be a whole animal skeleton or just a bone. It may be a whole forest of plants or just the imprint, like an outline, of a leaf. Sometimes even the footprints made by animals walking in mud become fossils.

HOW FOSSILS FORM

1. For a fossil to form, the animal or plant remains or trace must first be buried. An animal might drown in a river and sink to the bottom. The soft parts of its body will rot away, leaving just the bones and teeth.

2. Gradually, layers of silt and sand will cover it up. Over millions of years, the sediment will change into sedimentary rock and the bones will slowly dissolve away.

3. Minerals mixed in water will replace the bony material. Slowly, the animal remains will be replaced by solid rock.

4. Many years later, the fossils may be found at a cliff face or in a quarry. Scientists study such fossils to learn about Earth's ancient past.

PROJECT

Make your own fossil casts

You will need
Plaster of paris
A tray of sand
A shell

1. Press the shell into the tray of sand to make a clear imprint.

2. Mix the plaster of paris with some water to form a smooth paste.

3. Pour the mixture over the mark left in the sand.

4. Wait until the plaster has set hard.

5. Remove the plaster and examine your "fossil."

6. Try making fossils of leaves or bones. Make a cast of a real fossil if you have one.

FOSSIL FUELS

The main fuels that we use today come from the remains of living things. Coal is formed from the remains of plants that lived hundreds of millions of years ago. Oil and gas are formed from the remains of tiny sea creatures.

This fossilized fern was found in coal deposits.

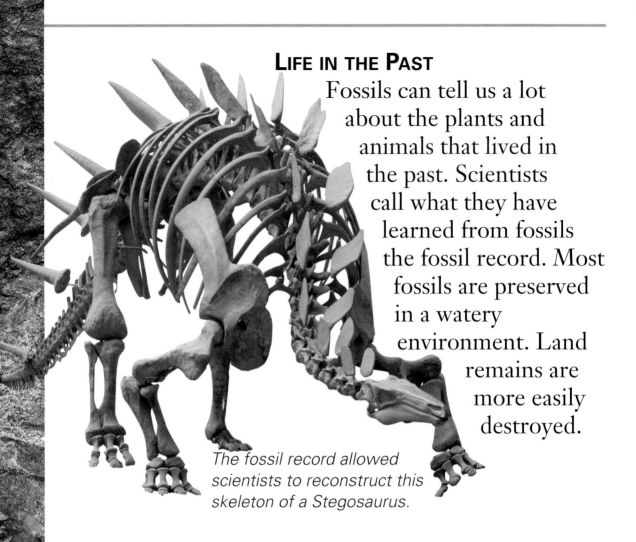

LIFE IN THE PAST

Fossils can tell us a lot about the plants and animals that lived in the past. Scientists call what they have learned from fossils the fossil record. Most fossils are preserved in a watery environment. Land remains are more easily destroyed.

The fossil record allowed scientists to reconstruct this skeleton of a Stegosaurus.

FOSSILIZED FOOTPRINTS

Fossilized dinosaur footprints can tell us about dinosaur behavior. Some dinosaurs lived in herds, while others lived on their own.

FEATHER FOSSILS

Archaeopteryx was a flying reptile that had feathers like a bird. This fossil and others tell scientists that birds probably evolved from reptiles.

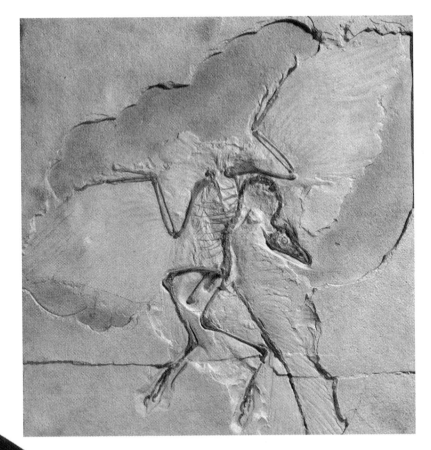

FOSSILS IN AMBER

Evergreen trees produce a sticky resin. Insects often become trapped in it. When this resin hardens, it is called amber. Insect fossils are often found in amber.

These insects are preserved in amber. The wasp was capturing a fly when they were both caught in the sticky resin.

USES OF ROCKS

One and a half million years ago, rocks were the most useful materials known to humans. That is why this period in history is known as the Stone Age. Stone Age people made tools and weapons from stones. By chipping away at a stone, usually a flint, they could make sharp tools such as hatchets, arrowheads, scrapers, and knife blades.

ROCK ART

Early artists used rocks containing iron to make a range of colors. They mixed each color with water or animal fat and painted onto cave walls.

BUILDING WITH ROCK

Rock has been used throughout history to build the structures people lived in.

Hundreds of years ago, castles were built by kings and lords as safe places to live. Castles had high towers so that soldiers could keep a lookout for enemies. The walls were thick to prevent attackers from breaking through. Most castles are over 500 years old. They were so well built that many still stand today.

BUILDINGS TODAY

Today we crush and mix all kinds of rocks to make many building materials. Glass, which is made from a mixture of sand, limestone, and soda ash, is also used in building. The buildings of today are often so extraordinary that it is difficult to remember that they are still made of rock.

COLLECTING ROCKS

It is not difficult to start your own rock collection. All you need is a small hammer, a magnifying glass, some safety glasses, and a bag to store your finds.

WHERE TO LOOK

Beaches are often good places to start looking for rocks. Beaches can be dangerous places, so always take an adult with you. Start by collecting rocks of different colors. Look at the rock through your magnifying glass. Are the crystals large or small? Test the hardness of the rock. Does it crumble easily in your hand, or do you need to hit it with your hammer? Always wear safety glasses when hammering rock, so that chips of rock don't fly in your eyes.

Wrap your finds carefully in paper. When you get home you can try to find them in a reference book. Your local library will have one of these. When you have found out what your rocks are, you can label them and store them in a display tray.

An egg carton makes a good display tray for small rocks.

FINDING FOSSILS

Find out where in your local area you might be able to find fossils. Most museums will have collections of rocks and fossils on display as well as information and reference books.

Ammonites are one of the most frequently found fossils. They are the remains of the hard shells of extinct sea creatures.

You may need to split rocks to remove your fossil sample. Be careful with your hammer. Chip gently so you do not damage your fossil. Remember, the fossil has been waiting millions of years for you to find it. It would be a shame to ruin it now!

Sometimes rock hunters make important discoveries. Start hunting—one day the discoverer could be you!

GLOSSARY

core The innermost part of Earth.

crust The thin, outer layer of Earth.

crystal A solid material that has flat sides, called faces.

fossil The remains or trace of a living thing that has been preserved in rock.

fossil fuel Fuels, such as coal or petroleum, made from the remains of organisms that lived millions of years ago.

igneous rock Solid rock formed within Earth by very great heat. This once molten rock has cooled and hardened.

mantle The layer of Earth between the crust and the core.

metal A mineral that is shiny and easily shaped.

metamorphic rock Rock that has changed form as the result of great heat or pressure.

meteorite A piece of rock from space that has fallen to Earth.

mineral A solid material that occurs naturally, is usually taken from the ground, and is not a living organism.

molten rock Hot, liquid rock.

ore A rock from which useful minerals can be removed.

sedimentary rock Rock formed from tiny particles that are moved and gathered by the activity of water, ice, or wind.

smelting The process of separating a metal from its ore by using heat.

FURTHER READING

Arnold, Caroline. *Trapped in Tar: Fossils from the Ice Age*. Clarion Books, 1994.

Bass, Lin. *Science Close-Up: Rocks*. (Deluxe Science Close-Up Kits series). Golden Books Family, 1995.

Baylor, Byrd. *Everybody Needs A Rock*. Simon and Schuster Childrens', 1985.

Chapman, Gillian, and Robson, Pam. *Art from Rocks and Shells*. (Salvaged! Series). Raintree Steck-Vaughn, 1995.

Christian, Spencer, and Felix, Antonia. *Is There a Dinosaur in Your Backyard? The World's Most fascinating Fossils, Rocks, and Minerals*. (Spencer Christian World of Wonders series). Wiley, 1998.

Lye, Keith. *Rocks and Minerals*. (What about…? series). Raintree Steck-Vaughn, 1992.

Pellant, Chris. *Rocks and Minerals*. (Fact Finders series). Random House Value, 1990.

Snedden, Robert. *Rocks and Soils*. (Science Projects series). Raintree Steck-Vaughn, 1998.

Alum. You may find hobby stores in your area that carry alum. Here is one source that you can contact. Hobbymasters, 42 White Street, Red Bank, NJ 07701. Phone (732) 842-6020. Website www.hobbymasters.com

The publishers would like to thank the following for permission to reproduce their pictures:

AKG: page 24, top, (Arnim Tolke); **Bruce Coleman:** page 6, (Jules Cowan), 7, top (P. Kaya), 12, bottom, (Dr. Frieder Sauer), 17, (Derek Croucher), 18, (Jules Cowan), 21, bottom (Norman Tomalin), 24, bottom. (Jan Taylor), 25, top, 26, top, (P. Kaya), cover (John Cancalosi); **Discovery Picture Library:** page 14, both; **Chris Fairclough;** page27, top, 28; **Gettyone Stone:** page 4, (Joe Cornish), 5, top, (Art Wolfe), bottom, (Hugh Sitton), 8, (Dennis Oda), 10, (Paul Harris), 11, (Steve Taylor), 15, top, (Mark Snyder), botom, (Ken Graham), 16, top, (Alan Klehr), bottom, (G. Brad Lewis), 20, (Trevor Wood), 21, top, (Grilly Bernard), 25, bottom, (Howard Grey), 26, bottom, (Philip & Karen Smith), 27, bottom, (William S. Helsel); **Science Photo Library**: page 7, top, (Sinclair Stammers), bottom, (Pekka Parvianinen), 12, top, Astrid & Hans-Frieder Michler, 23, (George Bernard); **Shropshire County Museum Service:** 29, bottom.

INDEX